THE BROWNINGS

BY
OLIVER ELTON
LL.D., D.LITT., F.B.A.
PROFESSOR OF ENGLISH LITERATURE IN THE
UNIVERSITY OF LIVERPOOL

HASKELL HOUSE PUBLISHERS LTD.
Publishers of Scarce Scholarly Books
NEW YORK. N. Y. 10012
1971

First Published 1924

HASKELL HOUSE PUBLISHERS LTD.
Publishers of Scarce Scholarly Books
280 LAFAYETTE STREET
NEW YORK, N. Y. 10012

Library of Congress Catalog Card Number: 71-169189

Standard Book Number 8383-1331-0

Printed in the United States of America

NOTE

This essay is a chapter, revised here for separate issue, from the writer's *Survey of English Literature, 1830–1880*, first published in 1920. A chronological table and brief notes on the literature of the subject are appended.

CONTENTS

		PAGE
I	Robert Browning: his social aspect and normality; love of history, fact, legend, and invention—Six phases of his poetry outlined	7
II	Long imperfect poems: *Pauline* and the *Essay* on Shelley; *Paracelsus*; *Sordello*	12
III	*Bells and Pomegranates*; note on plays; *Pippa Passes*	16
IV	Nos. iii. and vii. of *Bells and Pomegranates*, containing shorter pieces; Browning's true field—Narratives: *The Glove*—Romantic rebelliousness—Element of the grotesque; its varieties—Lyric gift .	21
V	*Christmas-Eve* and *Easter-Day*, Browning's principal confession of faith . .	26
VI	*Men and Women* (*i.e.* the 'fifty' so first named)—The poet's later classification—The eccentric again—Love poetry, its varieties and handicraft—The 'men and women' as later defined: dramatic monologue, usually in blank verse .	29
VII	*Dramatis Personæ*; a new strain; the verse of frustrated love—Poems with theses: *Gold Hair*—*Rabbi Ben Ezra* .	37
VIII	*The Ring and the Book*—Nature of the 'book'; how used—The six 'mundane' speeches; the five self-defences—Character and position of the poem .	42

CONTENTS

		PAGE
IX	More *apologias* at length: *Hohenstiel-Schwangau, Fifine at the Fair, Red Cotton Night-Cap Country, Inn Album*—Disquisition and fiction in verse, poetry intermittent	49
X	Refreshment with Greek themes: *Balaustion*, etc.—Also *La Saisiaz*, etc. . .	55
XI	*Dramatic Idyls*; a new form of the 'dramatic romance'—The four last volumes	59
XII	Browning's dealings with words; love of monosyllables; false stresses; metrical mastery nevertheless—His grammar; an example; its justification . . .	64
XIII	His non-poetical element—Philosophic verse; creation of characters and types; power greatest in lyric—His men and women—Neutral ground between prose and verse—Browning's quality . .	70
XIV	Mrs. Browning: life and literary record; faults to be expected. . . .	77
XV	Nature; and the Greek poets—False rhymes	82
XVI	*Sonnets from the Portuguese, Casa Guidi Windows, Aurora Leigh* . . .	86
	Chronological Table	91
	Notes	95

THE BROWNINGS

I

Robert Browning: his social aspect and normality; love of history, fact, legend, and invention. Six phases of his poetry outlined.

Irritable men of letters like Landor and Carlyle found to their relief that Robert Browning was unlike themselves, being in common intercourse hearty, normal, and unperturbed; a man who might have done well in law or diplomacy or any strong-headed profession. There was even a fancy that he had somewhere a private genius, or dæmon, who did his verses for him. In the Eighties, when many intellectual persons were adoring and explaining him, society remarked upon his easy suit of chain-armour, which kept the earnest souls at a courteous distance. This mundane behaviour was no mere defence in Browning, but well in keeping with his peculiar talent.

For it suits his thirst for hard and real situations, for history and Newgate annals, for the story of forgotten people ' of importance in their day '; in whose company, as in all companies, he moves so readily; they may be painters, thinkers, musicians, dreamers, politicians, fighters, lovers—especially lovers. However intricate and spiry a fabric he may raise, he likes to feel the firm rock beneath him, and to quarry out of it. Andrea del Sarto, and Pompilia, and Ned Bratts, and Miranda in *Red Cotton Night-Cap Country* had really existed in some such shape as he presents them. When he draws upon fiction and legend, for Ivàn Ivànovitch or Caliban, his aim is similar; it is to preserve keeping; he refuses to be untrue to the story and its associations. And when he invents, it is in the same spirit again; he wants to produce the illusion of fact and not the illusion of dreams —to be *right* about situation and motive, just as if he had history behind him. All this means a wide acquaintance with the big world, past and present, real and imaginary. Browning is a man of the world in this considerable sense of the term. He has been compared with some reason to a novelist; but he is more like a critic who tries to recover the features of past or alien minds and to recreate them faithfully. This, too, is the way of Walter Pater, otherwise so unlike Browning. The aim is to portray the spirit of Fra Lippo or Leonardo, of Marius or Karshish, in all its windings, in its setting of circumstance: the man in his habit as he lived. Browning makes the man speak for himself, always in some testing and critical situation (as Pater, indeed, points out). In his poems there is none of the stillness of the *Imaginary Portraits;* and the procedure, though perhaps not more difficult than the exquisite analysis of *Emerald Uthwart* or *Gaston*, brings us much nearer to life. Once more it has to be asked what Browning made of this gift, and into what moulds his invention fell.

His career as a poet falls into some six stages, which may be summarised as follows. 1. He begins with three long poems, *Pauline*, *Paracelsus*, and *Sordello*, which are full of confused wealth, but are cast into prolix and shapeless forms, plainly unworthy of such a talent. He also writes *Strafford*, his first play. 2. Then come the eight series of *Bells and Pomegranates*[n], containing seven plays, which are not exactly plays, but still show his talent clearing up magnificently. Browning is now in the thick of theatrical and literary society, a man of the world with many friends. But no writer of the time except his wife and possibly Carlyle, can be thought to have coloured his genius. In two other numbers of *Bells and Pomegranates* his true field, the shorter poem, the lyric or the monologue, is revealed. 3. His married life is the golden age of his genius and happiness. He lives in Italy, and is under its spell. He writes the long confession of faith, *Christmas Eve and*

Easter Day. Next come the fifty pieces, *Men and Women.* Browning's powers are now at their best, and are so to continue for some thirteen years. But meantime his production seems to be checked, first by his happiness and then by his bereavement; yet his honours are heightened and his command of grandeur is much more apparent when he at last produces *Dramatis Personæ.* 4. On *The Ring and the Book* Browning, as a master of the long poem, stands or falls, and surely stands. 5. He goes on writing, on a scale not so vast, but still generous. His powers, according to some, now begin to decline; but this must be only half-true, although the brains no doubt tend to overpower the poetry. There is much new invention and analysis, and no abatement of force, and often a new sweetness. There are the three volumes on Greek subjects, of which the finest is *Balaustion's Apology,* two metrical disquisitions, of which *Fifine at the Fair* is the more intelligible and poetical; and two criminal tales in verse, of which *The Inn Album* is the more sombre. In *La Saisiaz* he comes back to theology, in *The Two Poets of Croisic* to narrative, and in *Pacchiarotto* to the shorter poem. 6. In *Dramatic Idyls,* Browning has a *renouveau*; the old dramatic romance, or lyric, of his youth reappears with freshened colours. And his lyric flow is never quite dried up, in the four volumes that remain, from *Jocoseria* to *Asolando*. The good and great things may come more rarely, but there is the old strength and the old savour; and however much Browning may break the customs and even the laws of poetry, he is never safe against his own genius.

II

*Long imperfect poems : *Pauline* and the *Essay* on Shelley ; *Paracelsus : Sordello*.*

Shelley, the 'Sun-Treader,' had only been ten years dead when Browning, a youth barely of age, produced his *Pauline*, in which the vague flush of imagery and the fervent faintness of outline betray the ruling influence. Long afterwards, in 1852, Browning described the poet who had thus quickened his fancy. Shelley, he says, ranks high amongst those prophetic spirits, of the 'subjective' kind, who do not merely delineate life and their own minds in terms that appeal to mankind at large, but who see all things transcendentally. Such a spirit

is impelled to embody the thing he perceives, not so much with reference to the many below as to the one above him, the supreme Intelligence which apprehends all things in their absolute truth—an ultimate view ever aspired to, if but partially attained, by the poet's own soul. Not what man sees, but what God sees—the *Ideas* of Plato, seeds of creation lying burningly on the Divine Hand—it is towards these that he struggles.

So, Shelley's 'noblest and predominating characteristic' is

his simultaneous perception of Power and Love in the absolute, and of Beauty and Good in the concrete, while he throws, from his poet's station between both, swifter, subtler, and more numerous films for the connection of each with each, than have been thrown by any modern artificer of whom I have knowledge.

This is indeed ' seeing Shelley plain ' ; and we may guess that some such ambition came to be Browning's own—namely to interpret this earthly show of ' men and women,' with their mental histories, in the light of that loftier reference ; so that he remained, at bottom, a theologian, though a theologian *sui generis*, to the end. In the same essay he recognises that the ' subjective ' and ' objective ' elements may be variously mixed in one man ; and in himself they were thus mixed. His religion, or theodicy, colours his whole reading of life, and interpenetrates (to use a word of Shelley's own) his dramatic and lyrical studies. We may, then, safely expect to watch this union of elements as we pace once more the long gallery of Browning's works.

In *Paracelsus* the drawing is firmer, and the execution often splendid to the point of extravagance. But the whole is ill-shapen and diffuse, and afterwards Browning could have packed it all into a hundred lines. For one thing, the outer chronicle of the real Paracelsus, a true herald of medicine and chemistry despite his philosophic fantasies, is swamped by the fatally allusive style of narrative; nor is it clearly connected with the mental drama which is the true subject. Paracelsus aspires to know nature and God, and to help mankind. But mankind rejects him, and he is baffled, and dies after long struggle and delirium. Browning's ideal strain is already loud and clear, and there is remarkable richness in the lyrics; yet all is unrelieved and superabundant. Knowing the event, in *Paracelsus* we can now perceive the writer of *A Death in the Desert* or *Easter-Day*, though hardly the writer of *Pompilia* or of *Caliban upon Setebos*.

Few genuine poets have insulted art more strenuously than Browning does in *Sordello*. With an effort, the story can be made out; the thing has been done. But no comment and no undeniable oases can redeem *Sordello*. Dante, who had set the figure of the poet-patriot in the clear immortal light of his *Purgatory*, inspired Browning but failed to instruct him. Browning buried himself in the obscure history of the time, assumed that every one knew it, interwove it with the spiritual drama, treated it with all license, and so hid away Sordello himself in a dense thicket of allusion. Sordello is another baffled aspirant, with his hungry mind fixed on all life and knowledge for its prey. At last he perishes in a conflict between love and ambition. The conception deserves a better fate; but in spite of the flashes of beauty that flit over the scene whenever Palma, Sordello's love, appears, the poem suffocates itself.

III

Bells and Pomegranates; note on plays ; *Pippa Passes.*

Like Tennyson, Browning was a persistent 'maker of plays,' though he was never to conquer the theatre. *Strafford* was staged by Macready, *A Blot in the 'Scutcheon* by Phelps, and *Colombe's Birthday* by Helen Faucit; these pieces and others have been revived by enthusiasts. But the question to-day is how the eight dramas read, and not how they act. In each one of them can be found dramatic material and dramatic moments; none of them lack life, or poetry, or Browning's natural nobility of accent. Yet hardly one, unless it be *Colombe's Birthday*, is a satisfactory poem. They all show Browning working his path through drama towards monodrama, which is his real field, and in which he is meanwhile triumphing by the way. Play-writing disciplined his talent and taught him his method.

Strafford is full of energy ; and though it begins barely and drily, the poetry and pathos assert themselves in the final scenes, where Strafford listens to the singing of his children before he finally loses faith in his worthless master. The historians repudiate Browning's Pym, who distracts the interest and whose speeches little justify the awestruck allusions of the other characters to his voice and presence. Still we can see why Macready hailed the work in the lean years of the drama. Next came *Pippa Passes*, whose lyrical charm and tragic force it may seem insensate to resist. Browning, no doubt, must have all the honours of his unique conception. The little holidaying mill-girl lets herself dream that she is each in turn of 'Asolo's Four Happiest Ones'; passes the window of each, singing, at some critical instant in the fates of those within; awakens, being thus overheard, the remorse or resolve of each overhearer, so changing all the issues of their lives; and, on the last occasion, likewise saves herself, unawares, from an infamy contrived against her, and goes to sleep still singing. It must be said that four distinct conversions give us some pause; as for one or two, let them pass, and Pippa with them. But we are told to think that the child's song would perturb a very tough and horny Monsignore while he is engaged with his blackguard agent in a game of mutual blackmail. No doubt we are outside the world of fact all the time; but here there is too hard a clash between the worlds of criminal fiction and of didactic idyll. Still, in the most tragic scene of all, the 'bright-infernal' dialogue of Ottima and Sebald (which reminds us of Thomas Middleton's dramas), the poetic reason is convinced; for we are made ready for the violent revulsion of Sebald from his paramour, 'magnificent in sin'; and Pippa's singing, quite credibly, turns the scale.

In the plays that followed Browning practised many styles; now, in *King Victor and King Charles*, tracing tortuous intrigue and policy, in language very curt and stripped and also far too allusive; now, in *The Return of the Druses* (a much plainer story) bursting into impassioned Eastern figure, and striking out lines that flash like the Rhodian 'eight-point cross' or the tiara of the Hakeem; now, in *A Blot in the 'Scutcheon*, improvising a poor violent plot which repels the judgment, and for which the verse, often sweet and moving, is far too good. The young Tennysonian English girl, Lady Mildred, has been betrayed by the young Earl Mertoun; who, loving her nevertheless truly and wishing to make amends, next courts her openly, with the approval of her family; but still, incredibly, visits her window in the night. He is seen by her heroic brother Tresham, who kills him in duel; Mildred dies and Tresham poisons himself. Browning disdained to invent any such story afterwards. Very different is *Colombe's Birthday*; he has left no drama better plotted, none where the threads of romantic and chivalrous interest are more nicely interwoven. It might be called a political idyll. The verse is unusually simple and beautiful, and the various styles of poetic eloquence well match the speakers—Colombe, Duchess of Cleves and Verviers, threatened with expulsion; Berthold, the claimant, ambitious and unscrupulous, capable of magnanimity but not of love; and Valens, the advocate of Cleves, the winner at last of the Duchess in reward for his loyalty and self-denial.

Next came two plays of historical cast but not founded upon history. In *A Soul's Tragedy* there is excellent odd prose, spoken by the legate Ogniben, who is a sort of pocket Machiavelli; and there is one of Browning's favourite studies of a slippery character. But there is not enough in Chiappino to support the interest. He is man enough to be ready to die for his friend Luitolfo by shouldering the guilt of Luitolfo's tyrannicide, but not man enough to forego the profit when the crime turns out to be glorious and popular. In *Luria*, despite the crowd of long-winded speeches, there is more substance and imagination. Luria the Moor is one of Browning's heroic figures, and well matched with his adversary Tiburzio as Shakespeare's Coriolanus is with Aufidius. He has the passionate loyalty of the East; his magnanimity is coldly used and betrayed by the city of Florence which he has saved. Her treachery breaks his heart and he takes poison. There is a certain deliberate splendour about the language of this play, and in more than one passage can be heard the large Elizabethan style ; with a difference indeed, but it is hardly mistakable :

Oh world, where all things pass and nought abides,
Oh life, the long mutation—is it so ?
Is it with life as with the body's change ?
—Where, e'en tho' better follow, good must pass,
Nor manhood's strength can mate with boy-
    hood's grace,
Nor age's wisdom, in its turn, find strength,
But silently the first gift dies away,
And though the new stays, never both at once.

IV

Nos. iii. and vii. of *Bells and Pomegranates*, containing shorter pieces ; Browning's true field—Narratives : *The Glove*—Romantic rebelliousness—Element of the grotesque ; its varieties—Lyric gift.

From the first it must have been clear to the wise, though not to the official critics, that in all these dramas and lengthy works there was much ore, and that only crushing and refining—only that, but an infinite deal of that—was required ; and also that Browning, in his shorter poems, had achieved this process already. Quite early he had begun to find the right shape for his compositions. Shape mattered even more than style, because it usually carried style along with it. In 1836 were printed *Porphyria's Lover* and *Johannes Agricola in Meditation*. The former would have pleased Baudelaire ; and Browning was always to like a clinical subject. From his vantage-ground of healthy sense he reached out a hand of lively sympathy—dramatic sympathy—towards villainy, crime, and craziness of all kinds, the more curious and piquant the better. Herein, by the way, lies the strength of his much-deplored 'optimism.' The faith that could survive the task of creating the alchemist in *The Laboratory* or Guido Francheschini or the 'elder man' in *The Inn Album* is proof against anything. Such a writer cannot be accused, like a sentimentalist, of not facing the worst. Still, in his early verse pathology does not rule, and the strain is lyrical and romantic.

It is clear now, though it was less clear at the time, how safely English poetry had been re-established by Tennyson and Browning by the year 1845. The third and seventh bunches of *Bells and Pomegranates*[n] comprise about thirty lyrical or narrative poems, none of them lengthy. Many of Browning's future powers and interests are here represented. The lyrics are not all stories, but the stories are all 'lyrical ballads,' and of a novel kind. Already is to be noticed the poet's habit of giving an extra turn to the ethical screw. He must have a problem in casuistry; must dissect the behaviour of a man in some crisis that is just too strong, or just not too strong, for his moral resources. This is seen in *The Glove*, where we are told that 'Peter Ronsard *loquitur*.' But that poet would not have picked the story to pieces, or have urged that a true lover would never have thought twice about the wanton offence of his lady in sending him into the lion-pit after her glove; nor would he afterwards have married the knight unhappily

to a king's leman, and the lady happily to a page.
Browning was to sift such problems more sternly
in his *Dramatic Idyls*, long afterwards.

Two other characteristics are clear in the thirty
poems. Browning gives a fresh turn to the old
romantic mood of rebellion. Anything to be
free! *The Flight of the Duchess* is an utterance
of the longing for escape which is also heard in
Youth and Art; or in the tale of Jules and Phene.
Go off to the gypsies, like the Duchess, or to a
garret and live on love, or to 'some unsuspected
isle in the far seas!' Go with your mate, your
lover, and damn the consequences, for 'God's
in his Heaven!' There is something of Blake
in this; and there was plenty of wild sap
in the youthful Browning, who himself ran off
with his wife, most successfully. The refine-
ments of a deep and serious union, the 'silent
silver lights and darks undreamed-of,' are sub-
sequent; Browning is their poet also. Further,
these early pieces deal much in the grotesque.
The Boy and the Angel, with its pure sort of
Tennysonian beauty, is exceptional. And the
grotesque, whether it minister to the sublime,
or to the picturesque, or simply to irony, is
naturally signalled by the metre. Browning's
acrobatic skill in queer rhyming, which led him
to some of his worst failures and of his greatest
successes, must have encouraged this tendency.
It is purely impish and childlike in *The Pied*

Piper of Hamelin, the story of which he found in his father's library, in Wanley's *Wonders of the Little World*. The scene has often been painted, but the rhymes cannot be painted. The *Soliloquy of the Spanish Cloister* exhibits, like the *Memoir* of Mark Pattison, the uncouth and fearful joy of monastic or academic hatreds. *Sibrandus Schafnaburgensis* is pure fun. *The Englishman in Italy*, though not exactly grotesque, is homely and joyous, with a joy as of treading the wine-vat, and the rhymes lift it easily into the higher strain. *The Flight of the Duchess*, with its somersaulting verses and its tumbles into rank imagery, is Browning's greatest feat in the grotesque, prior to *Caliban upon Setebos*. And the grotesque, in such hands, implies not absence of form but precision of humorous strangeness in form; and it need not exclude, though it may be content to do without, beauty of treatment.

Some of the pieces in *Bells and Pomegranates* cannot be classified. *Waring* is all pictures and no story, a lyrical fantasy prompted by the writer's memories of his friend Alfred Domett. Domett's own poem *Ranolf and Amohia, A South-Sea Daydream* (1872) contains some sub-tropical scenery and idyllic passages of a simple beauty. But Waring also embodies the desire for escape with no certain bourne in view. The other items in the two volumes might be set in a kind of scale, according as they approach more or less closely to pure song. The resurgence of English lyric is assured in *The Lost Mistress*, in *Meeting at Night*, and in 'Nay, but you who do not love her.' The *Cavalier Tunes, Through the Metidja to Abd-el-Kadr*, and *How they Brought the Good News* are without subtleties; they are all drums and horse-hoofs, and are all magnificent. In *Rudel to the Lady of Tripoli* the verse advances soft and smooth like the ship that bore the dying troubadour to his lady. Heine had already touched the story, and Carducci was to tell it again (1888); but our reluctant language, which could yield the cadence of

The far, sad waters, Angel, to this nook!

is not overmatched even by the vowelled Italian:

—Contessa, che è mai la vita?
È l'ombra d'un sogno fuggente.
La favola breve è finita,
Il vero immortale è l'amor.
  Aprite le braccia al dolente.
Vi aspetto al novissimo bando.
Ed or, Melisenda, accomando
A un bacio lo spirto che muor.

V

Christmas-Eve and *Easter-Day*, Browning's principal confession of faith.

Browning in 1850 produced *Christmas-Eve* and *Easter-Day*, his fullest though not his final confession of faith. It was the year of *In Memoriam*. Not long before Marian Evans had translated Strauss's *Leben Jesu*, and Newman had published his *Development of Christian Doctrine*. For once the backwash of contemporary thought reached Browning. Though packed with curious lore, he seems to have had no special training in the philosophy of his own or of other times. Philosophy? To him philosophy and religion were all but the same; and in this, if in little else, he was mediævally-minded. His imagination was now touched by these extremes of religion which he knew best, the Protestant in its densest vulgarity, and the Roman at the summit of its ritual. To neither of these is he bound, and his reason reacts against them both; but he asks what is their common measure and saving element, and he finds it in the principle of love. But love is absent, or only a phantom, in the cult of the German professor, the high mild enthusiast, who worships the critical destroying reason and leaves the divinity and almost the reality of Christ a myth. Browning writes as if there could be no religion of love or 'humanity' outside the Christian pale. *Christmas-Eve* is a poem of curious mark and workmanship. The three scenes of the chapel, the basilica, and the lecture-hall, in which the grotesque and the sublime are variously blended, are bound together, partly by the poet's reasonings, and partly by the vision of Christ; who guides the speaker, either in the body or the spirit, through the long journey, and upon whose figure his final faith and love converge. In the end he gets back to the chapel and is left joining humbly in the hymn. The pictures of the moon-rainbow and of the mass are among Browning's greatest. That of the meeting-house is in the most vivid of doggerel; and this element is allowed to infect the whole work. Much of *Christmas-Eve* is religion in Hudibrastics, with a touch of *Christabel* thrown in. *Easter-Day* is in level short couplets with hardly a touch of oddity and with one burst of splendour—the vision of judgment that gives the key to the poem. In the main dialogue two nameless speakers argue and instruct each other; it is not too clear whether they express the poet's own conviction or a more or less dramatic mood. The tone is not catholic and comprehensive as in *Christmas-Eve*, but exclusive and austere. Even the soundest joys of earth and the highest thoughts of man are subordinate to the single-minded service of God. Yet these solicitations of humanity, it is conceded, are steeped from the first in the principle of love; for they too are 'service.' For the later forms of Browning's theology we turn to *Rabbi Ben Ezra*, *A Death in the Desert*, *Abt Vogler*, and *La Saisiaz*; and there, though essentially the same, his faith and 'optimism' are less rigidly exacting. The bareness or blankness of style which marks many of them is prefigured in *Easter-Day*.

VI

Men and Women (*i.e.* the 'fifty' so first named)
—The poet's later classification—The eccentric
again—Love poetry, its varieties and handicraft—The 'men and women' as later defined:
dramatic monologue, usually in blank verse.

In that Monte Cristo cave-treasure, the volumes
of 1855 entitled *Men and Women*, all Browning's
former gifts and themes reappear, now greatly
enriched and varied. Every poem in them would
deserve a review. Classification is difficult; nor
can Browning's own be pressed. The *Men and
Women* of 1855 consist of the 'fifty poems
finished' together with the dedication *One Word
More*. But these, in 1863, were combined with
the non-dramatic pieces taken from *Bells and
Pomegranates*, and the collection thus formed was
sifted out under the three classes of 'dramatic
lyrics,' of 'dramatic romances,' and lastly of
'men and women' in the narrower sense. Only
twelve poems (afterwards increased by one) now
bore that title, most of them being dramatic
monologues which are neither strictly lyrical
nor narrative. But the distribution could not
be precise; nor does Browning's poetry ever fit
well into compartments. *My Last Duchess*

figures among 'romances,' but it belongs to 'men and women' every whit as much as the *Epistle* of Karshish. *Mesmerism* and *The Last Ride Together* are also called romances, but if a romance must be a story, they have not much story. The lyric *Rudel* is placed, on the other hand, amongst the twelve 'men and women.' I shall not keep to Browning's classes, but only trace one or two of the patterns that run through the whole shining fabric up to this date.

His deliberate queerness, to begin with, is as rampant as ever, and it has to find fresh excuses for existing. In *Holy-Cross Day* it is a foil to the solemnity of the concluding march. In *The Heretic's Tragedy* it is there chiefly to enjoy itself—an excellent reason. In *A Grammarian's Funeral* the grotesque is used in the service of grandeur. The rhyming feats (*cock-crow, rock row*; *fabric, dab brick*) echo the broken step of the climbers, and also their recital, half-defiant, half-affectionate, of the dead scholar's purposes, in the world's eye, so puerile. The poem presages the gaunter style of *Dramatis Personæ*, and the Grammarian ennobles the gospel of minute 'research' as surely as George Eliot's caricature of it in Mr. Casaubon leaves that faith piteous and futile. But, to Browning, the faith is the thing; faith with whatever object, and faith which in this life may at once fail of its full object and miss the common joys of life. The doggerel

in *Old Pictures in Florence* denotes, I suppose, a
snap of the fingers at the world's forgetfulness of
the good obscure painters who have thought
only of the work and not of the praise. And in
A Pretty Woman half the bitterness against the
soulless beauty of the lady would be missed,
without the touch of oddness and the slippery
dexterous dactyls :

> Shall we burn up, tread that face at once
>   Into tinder
>   And so hinder
> Sparks from kindling all the place at once ?
>
> Or else kiss away one's soul on her ?
>   Your love-fancies !
>   —A sick man sees
> Truer, when his hot eyes roll on her !

These effects are not rare in Browning's love-
poetry, which is endless in variety and in which he
breaks away from all tradition. No abandoned
romanticist, he well knows, like Johnson and
Shakespeare, that 'love is but one of many
passions'; his grammarian, his rabbi, his saints,
stand outside love in the ordinary sense. Yet
his own hopes for mankind and much of his
religious faith are heavily staked upon his gospel
of love. Were that to prove illusory, what would
be left of the 'optimist' ? Once, late in life,
in *Ferishtah's Fancies*, he shivers at such a
possibility :

Only, at heart's utmost joy and triumph, terror
  Sudden turns the blood to ice: a chill wind disencharms
All the late enchantment! What if all be error—
  If the halo irised round my head were, Love, thine arms?

This, again, is only a mood. Browning seldom betrays a doubt about the revelation of love: a subject on which he muses with all possible sympathy and curiosity, concerning himself with strange cases and conjectures, and, like Meredith, returning to the notion that love is not only man's chief happiness but his chief ordeal. Some of these poems are rapidly flashed pictures, like *Meeting at Night* and *My Star*. Some of the most deeply considered give the feminine point of view; in *A Woman's Last Word* and *Any Wife to Any Husband* there is the tone of piercing sadness and resignation. Some turn on a favourite idea, the capture or loss of the mystical moment, the one chance by which the union of spirits may be sealed. In *Cristina* (1842) the chance is caught but lost again, as it is in *Two in the Campagna*. In *A Lover's Quarrel* it is triumphantly recaptured. In *The Statue and the Bust* it slips away through cowardice; in *Respectability* the world is defied and happiness gained, through courage. *By the Fireside* reveals the secret won: 'the forests had done it'; and this poem may reflect, as *One Word More* avowedly does, a personal experience. Browning did not love only in verse, or by dramatic sympathy; much of his best writing of this kind dates from his married life. In *Love Among the Ruins*, one of his securest masterpieces, the sight of the old relics and the vision of the dead fighters and charioteers do not (as in some poem of Mr. Thomas Hardy's they might just as convincingly do) lay a cold hand upon the lover; but they make his happiness seem the compensation, or 'Earth's returns,' for those departed splendid vanities.

These love-poems, now more than half a century old, last perfectly well. They have no models, they are all quite different, and their handicraft is consummate. They are 'concise and perfect work.' There are rough edges to them, but there is no untidy dust or surplusage; and they sound, despite the poet's peculiar idiom, like natural speech; verse propagating verse, as it does in Shakespeare, and the poem never seeming to be thought out beforehand. Browning likes to invent measures, especially curt abrupt ones, which have this air of unstudied impassioned speech shaking itself without effort into rhyme :

> When I sewed or drew,
>   I recall
> How he looked as if I sung,
>   —Sweetly too.

> If I spoke a word,
>   First of all
> Up his cheek the colour sprung,
>   Then he heard.

More intricate are the fervent and lovely chimes of *Women and Roses*. But at whichever end we begin, whether with the impassioned thought or with the technique, we reach the same point of fusion between them. How often we are launched on the music of Swinburne and reach no thought at all; and how often, by the later Browning, we are launched on the thought and find no right expression for it! But that is no matter, when he has left us the 'fifty poems finished.'

Most of the thirteen pieces finally styled *Men and Women* are in blank verse; but it is of no monotonous pattern. Joyous and free in *Fra Lippo Lippi*, it is faint and dreamy and loth to finish in *Andrea del Sarto*; and in *The Bishop Orders his Tomb* it is broken and tessellated. Blank verse became the usual medium for the dramatic monologue, that form in which Tennyson and Rossetti and others excel, but of which Browning is the master. It is an exacting form, for the monologue has to tell the whole story, and also to reveal the character of other persons beside the speaker, in a natural way. In *Andrea del Sarto, called 'The Faultless Painter,'* which is all silver-grey and pathos, this feat is accomplished.

Andrea is resigned at once to the doom of a too perfect finish in his art, and to the faithlessness of the wife-model whose love, had it existed, might have made of him a Raphael. *Cleon*, a new kind of 'Hellenic,' in which the verse is remarkably stately and finished, has its pathos too, and its problem: Can the pagan artist, in his old age, live merely on his fame, and also on his sharpened sympathy with the youthful life which he cannot, in the flesh, enjoy? Cleon dreams of 'some future state revealed to us by Zeus,' and has heard of the insane doctrine on the subject preached by one Christus and one Paulus, who are perhaps the same person. A similar idea is developed in *The Strange Medical Experience of Karshish*. Here the Eastern scenery and detail are given with extraordinary gusto, and the 'transformation of all values' in the mind of the risen Lazarus is described in Browning's subtlest style. One of the most finished of these monologues is *How it Strikes a Contemporary*; it is intensely coloured, and every stroke tells; and above all, like *My Last Duchess*, it is short, and escapes the prolixity which from first to last is Browning's besetting and fatal danger. The 'contemporary' is the man in the street at Valladolid; what 'strikes' him is the figure of a poet, a kind of Browning, who sees everything and says nothing, and who becomes the legend and (unlike Browning) the terror of the place.

The full savour of the verse is felt in lines like these :

We merely kept a governor for form,
While this man walked about and took account
Of all thought, said and acted, then went home,
And wrote it fully to our Lord the King
Who has an itch to know things, He knows why,
And reads them in His bed-room of a night.

Bishop Blougram's Apology is mostly written in a style which does not encourage poetry. Blougram is the half-believing cleric who builds an argumentative house of cards in order to justify his retention of his stall and of his ' sphere of usefulness.' The figure is partially modelled on that of Wiseman, who reviewed Browning in the *Rambler* and dealt him a *coup de patte* which rather misses its mark : ' If Mr. Browning is a man of will and action, and not a mere dreamer and talker, we should never feel surprise at his conversion.' The poem is too long, and anticipates the pedestrian blank verse of the poet's later years. It also shows his fondness for letting an ambiguous or shady personage put his case to the utmost. All these, he says, are ' utterances of so many imaginary persons, and not mine ' ; all, that is, except the *One Word More* addressed to his wife, a poem written in London, but Italian in scenery, and moulded, for once, upon the pure line and colouring of Italian verse.

VII

Dramatis Personæ; a new strain; the verse of frustrated love—Poems with theses: *Gold Hair—Rabbi Ben Ezra*.

In *Dramatis Personæ*, which came out three years after Browning's bereavement, there is a sharper irony, a harder realism, and a higher grandeur than ever yet. The language is stiffer and more elliptical; there are more monosyllabic lines, knots of harsh consonants, and jingling internal rhymes. These devices, which became the prey of the parodist, are often used to express bitterness, just as Shakespeare's 'puns' on the lips of Queen Margaret or Lady Macbeth give the effect of a mock grin or *rictus*. The gayer variety of the style is seen in *Dis aliter Visum:*

> A match 'twixt me, bent, wigged and lamed,
>   Famous, however, for verse and worse,
> Sure of the Fortieth spare Arm-chair
>   When gout and glory seat me there,
> So, one whose love-freaks pass unblamed.

This later vein of grotesqueness recurs in *A Likeness*, in *Youth and Art*, and in the Morgue-poem *Apparent Failure*. Another variety of it pervades *Mr. Sludge, the Medium*, in which the poet relieves his mind of his cherished disgust at the practices which had impressed Mrs. Browning. The poem would bear separately reprinting to-day (1924), when there is some recrudescence of Sludge. In the religious satire *Caliban upon Setebos* eccentricity of form is used in yet another spirit; and the effect is so good as to make us forget that Shakespeare's own ' monster ' is not eccentric at all but acts and thinks quite naturally according to monster-law. Browning's grotesquerie is like some odd-shaped cactus, full of bristles, and more expressive than beautiful, but sometimes breaking, for the benefit of the connoisseur, into a morbid, red, and startling blossom. The most highly wrought poem of this class is *James Lee's Wife*, a series of nine speeches addressed to the fickle husband, all *staccato* in diction, but all charged with beauty and pathos. None of these poems except *Caliban* and *A Death in the Desert* are theological. *The Worst of It* and *Too Late* are purely human and dramatic. Others partly depend for their value on the argument.

And in one of them the argument is monstrous. *Gold Hair : A Story of Pornic* tells of the Breton girl with the wonderful tresses, massed by her own hand so strangely on her deathbed and by her request interred with her untouched. A piece, it might seem, of touching vanity ; but no, one of the Seven Sins was behind it ! The coffin, opened long afterwards, was found to be full of gold coins which had been hoarded in the hair. 'Why I deliver this horrible verse?' inquires the poet of himself. Why, because the Christian faith, which had been recently attacked in print, was the first or the only faith that 'taught Original Sin, The Corruption of Man's Heart.' Monstrous, I repeat. Such a conclusion requires the sin of a Judas or a Guido Franceschini to support it. Browning, well as he tells his tale, tells it like any naïf old priest—not, indeed, like the priest in the poem who built an altar out of the proceeds of the coffin-gold. The spectre of nineteenth-century criticism also haunts, rather unfairly, the last hours of St. John, in *A Death in the Desert*; but that poem is a lofty though terribly lengthy statement of Browning's conception of human progress, as at once limited and advanced by the conditions of this life. The language and cadence often recall Tennyson's in such lines as

Stung by the splendour of a sudden thought

or

Like the lone desert-bird that wears the ruff.

Along with Swinburne's *Hertha*, Browning's *Rabbi Ben Ezra* is the greatest metaphysical poem of his generation. Its power lies in the expression of a lofty austere ideal by means of a series of dazzling and glowing images. The wisdom of age recovers the poetry though not the pulse of youth. The loss of youth and of its joy is repaid by an increase of vision, and of the power to use the memories of youth for the ends of the soul. Life has lasted long enough for the Divine Potter to finish the cup that He is moulding; and therefore, 'let death complete the same':

> Look not thou down but up!
>   To uses of a cup,
> The festal board, lamp's flash and trumpet's peal,
>   The new wine's foaming flow,
>   The Master's lips aglow!
> Thou, heaven's consummate cup, what needst thou with earth's wheel?

Music is yet another avenue to the apprehension of goodness and beauty; this idea is set forth in *Abt Vogler*, with its heavily undulating harmonies, in which Browning's lyrical powers are seen at their utmost pitch. The whole volume of *Dramatis Personæ* marks the summit of his speculative verse, just as the volume of *Men and Women* shows to the full his mobility and humanity. But his power to compose a big poem, dramatic in essence though not in form, is tested for the first and last time in *The Ring and the Book*.

Browning had already produced many wonderful short pieces and some unsatisfactory long ones. He had written of love and religion, of painting and music, and of Italy. He had enlarged the scope of the poetical-grotesque. He had played at his ease upon the instrument of blank verse for the purposes of narrative, description, and reasoning. Where, then, should he display all these powers and interests at once and uncramped, and on the greater scale? Where find what Tennyson had failed to find in Arthur, and what Morris was almost to find in Sigurd, a subject that was not only great in itself, but great for *him*? Was he only to be remembered for those wonderful short things?

VIII

The Ring and the Book—Nature of the 'book'; how used—The six 'mundane' speeches; the five self-defences—Character and position of the poem.

Browning, at any rate, was sure that he had found his subject in the little 'yellow book' describing an old Roman murder case of the year 1698. The book is a sheaf of documents partly in print and partly in manuscript. They are in Latin and Italian, official and unofficial, pro and con; a chance-collection of papers, precious but incomplete, made by somebody, and in no other sense a book. One other pamphlet, outside this sheaf, Browning found and also used. The broken-down Count Guido Franceschini of Arezzo after committing many other villainies caused the murder of his wife Pompilia, aged seventeen, and of her alleged parents the Comparini couple. In defence he urged her adultery, which was maintained on the strength of forged letters, with the priest Giuseppe Caponsacchi. This friend had in fact helped her to fly from the house of torture: which affair had been dealt with indecisively in a previous lawsuit.

The 'book' contains the pleas and counter-pleas of counsel; summaries of evidence on either side, including oral depositions by Pompilia Caponsacchi, and others; the official sentence on Guido, who was duly convicted, and, upon the rejection of his appeal by Pope Innocent the Twelfth, executed; and further, some irresponsible unsigned tracts written on either side. This was Browning's lump of ore; and in one of his liveliest pages he tells how he found it on a Roman bookstall, mused on it, moulded it, refined it, and after four years of labour spurted on it the final acid, so driving out the alloy,

Till, justifiably golden, rounds my ring :

—the Ring, which receives its 'posy' of dedication to his 'lyric love,' now for seven years lost to him on earth.

The old book gives the story from various points of view; and these the poet increases to eleven or twelve, weaving in hundreds of scattered details from the record. But he finds that neither in book nor poem can such a story, or any story, ever be truly told. Not the passionless Pope, not the author, can ever say the last word. The eleven versions offered are all colourable, but they are incompatible. So we see that truth is elusive—that is, man's truth; only by circling round it, by watching facet after facet of it, can we see, and then in just outline,

God's own truth concerning that far-off Newgate episode. This eternal truth may be roughly recognised by human justice and countersigned by the official deputy of God upon earth. But such justice, though it may do its work at the time, cannot restore Pompilia; nor can it keep alive her memory, which is buried away in the old yellow papers. So it is for the poet to re-quicken the story; and had art, he thinks, ever a rarer enterprise—art, which does not simply republish, but also illuminates? And Browning then invents his peculiar method. Henry James sketched the story of *The Ring and the Book*[n] as a possible novel, with Caponsacchi for the central figure; it remains for some one to conceive it as a play. It would, I think, be a play in which prose and verse were mingled.

For six out of the eleven narratives are prosaic in their very intention; they are on the strictly worldly level, giving the gossip of Rome, or else the bare lawyer-facts of the case as discoloured by lawyer-rhetoric. The sections entitled 'Half-Rome,' 'The Other Half-Rome,' '*Tertium Quid*,' and 'The Book and the Ring' are built up from the scattered documents; while the speeches of the two counsel are taken, often verbally and consecutively, Latin tags and all, from their originals. The use of verse for this kind of work raises curious questions. No doubt it is the verse that carries us through, where prose might have wearied us—*quod lucro ponatur*, as Dominus Hyacinthus might have said. But then the result is neither poetry nor prose, but something between, yielding a very mixed kind of pleasure. One of the depositions, that of the serving-maid who describes the horrors of Guido's household, is put into the level prosaic verse afterwards used in *The Inn Album*. And throughout Browning's power of tessellation is surprising. Names, dates, incidents, and phrases of his original are inlaid without effort, though with some effect of bewilderment. No great historical novel or drama has kept closer to the material. Perhaps the true justification of this method is the picture which is built up before us, touch by touch, of the hard old cruel Roman world, with its jokes and flying scandal and its taste in oratory, and which is also a background for the redeeming figures of the girl, the priest, and the Pope.

There remain the speeches of these three and the two speeches of Guido. The yellow book, which is mostly bare in diction, shows unusual feeling when it chronicles the evidence given by those who saw Pompilia's last hours. These persons were greatly moved by her patience and goodness; and here is the germ of the poet's exalted reading of her character. Pompilia's own deposition in the 'book' is a plain tale told with dignity. She just lives long enough to tell it, and dies leaving her infant of two months behind her. She had heard, she depones, that Caponsacchi was a 'resolute' man, and had gone to him as a last hope. Browning said that he had found all of his Pompilia 'in the book.' In fact, he embodies everything that is in the book—her childish shifts and rages, her drugging of Guido and drawing of the sword upon him; but he also softens and glorifies it all; with some loss, it may be, of the convincing effect of the real Pompilia's story. More safely, he widens her vision and intelligence out of all recognition, making her love for the unborn or just born Gaetano the mainspring of her action.

He also invents the purged and spiritual love between Pompilia and Caponsacchi, by which an average light ecclesiastic is turned into a St. George or a Perseus. The description of this new birth of Caponsacchi, when he first sees Pompilia with her 'great, grave, griefful air,' standing at her window, is one of Browning's achievements. The unlettered Roman girl becomes the voice of his ideal conception of marriage, which he had so often expounded, but never in simpler or higher terms. As for Guido, in the yellow documents, he does not speak at all, except through the lips of partisans and lawyers. Here, then, Browning was unfettered. Still the sophistry of Guido's first oration in the poem is quite in keeping with the facts. Nor is there in the yellow book any comment from the

Pope; he is heard of as urging on the trial, and as overruling a plea for delay of sentence. In the poem he reviews the case, confirms the sentence, makes his own last account with heaven, and becomes the spokesman of something like Browning's own theology. He also comes out as a satirist and poet. He shows plenty of irony and scorn before he reaches, not too soon, his superb coronation of Pompilia and of the 'warrior-priest.' The Pope becomes Dantesque in temper though by no means in form:

Such denizens o' the cave now cluster round
And heat the furnace sevenfold: time indeed
A bolt from heaven should cleave roof and clear
  place,
Transfix and show the world, suspiring flame,
The main offender, scar and brand the rest,
Hurrying, each miscreant to his hole: then flood
And purify the scene with outside day—
Which yet, in the absolutest drench of dark,
Ne'er wants a witness, some stray beauty-beam
To the despair of hell.

The whole poem culminates in his last words; he sees no chance for Guido save in some unlikely miracle that may bring him to 'see, one instant, and be saved.' But Browning's next great stroke is to risk an anticlimax, and also escape it, by following at once with the second speech, the great eruption, of Guido, now condemned, a lost but shameless soul. One of the old documents assigns a much more edifying end to Guido; but the poet will have none of that. Then, with another deliberate drop, he adds a satiric epilogue; but at the end he recovers, and delivers his mind on the vital mission of the artist, the ring-maker, the truth-refiner, such as he has tried to prove himself. Once we grasp this bold and successful arrangement of *The Ring and the Book*, we can imagine no other.

When all is said it is one of the best, and not merely one of the strangest, poems of the last century. It is not in the Latin taste; the architecture is too eccentric, the ornament is too profuse and whimsical. Our ancestors would have called it a Gothic production. But we must leave Browning his own plan. His true subject is the contrast between Heaven and Hell, with the world's voices clamouring all around them and confounding their borders.

IX

More *apologias* at length: *Hohenstiel-Schwangau,
Fifine at the Fair, Red Cotton Night-Cap Country,
Inn Album*—Disquisition and fiction in verse,
poetry intermittent.

Browning, now enamoured of the long verse
apologia, practised it steadily for some years
more. He became a kind of metrical Balzac.
He much admired the creator of Vautrin and
of Louis Lambert. He has the same interest
in crime, in ambiguous characters, and in genius
that is very nearly mad. He has just as strong,
though not so gross, a digestion; he worships
goodness when it comes, but he loves to let a
scoundrel put his case and make his points. His
optimism and idealism are always ready to break
in, and though the result is not always poetry,
still poetry is always breaking in too. In Balzac
its place is taken by a thousand *pensées* concerning male and female nature and social
phenomena. The large-scale *apologia* is only
an expansion of Browning's favourite form.
Poisoners and dukes and murderers and bishops
had already had a hearing, the fullest having
been granted, so far, to Guido. But the 'mod-

ern Don Juan' and the 'saviour of society' talk through whole volumes, and the 'elder man' in the *Inn Album* cannot complain of the hour-glass. The result is not always tedious.

The earliest and most sawdusty poem of this group is *Prince Hohenstiel-Schwangau, Saviour of Society*. It had been drafted years before Napoleon the Third lay sick at Chislehurst; and thus, though published in 1871, it does not allude to his downfall. Browning did not share his wife's admiration for the opportunist visionary, and shared still less the fierce attitude of Victor Hugo. His half-imaginary prince spins a spider's web of self-excuse for the great gulf between his theories and his behaviour. The streak of idealism is true to history, but otherwise the 'prince' is little akin to the real emperor. And the construction of the poem is wantonly confusing. The overture, which at first seems to be describing facts, turns out to have been only a dream. Then the shuttle flies in bewildering fashion between what the speaker did, and what he might have done, and what others think, or might have thought, about his doings. The result is a long intricate sophism cut into the blankest of iambics.

In *Fifine at the Fair* Browning reverts to rhyme, and lightens the lumbering trot of Drayton's old Alexandrine couplet, and gets out of it a few long smooth gallops over the sward. His Don Juan is neither sombre nor delightedly cruel, but just a man who inveterately hunts for experience. Don Juan walks through the fair with Elvire, and proclaims her the perfect type of wife; and for the time he is in earnest. He sets her high above the gypsy Fifine, the newest of all the endless fair women—Helen, Cleopatra, and the rest—who have lured his imagination. He argues and refines on the matter interminably —and at last he goes off to Fifine, with an obvious lie to Elvire upon his lips. Much of Juan's harangue is a weariness; but the book is remarkable for the beauty of its similes, in which the poetry takes refuge, and which are almost of the length of parables. Also there are the lovely Breton landscapes of cliff and foreshore; and the plash of the waters gets into the verse. In the lyrical prologue and epilogue, the one gay and gracious, the other curt and elliptical, the double strain of the poem is repeated.

The facts of *Red Cotton Night-Cap Country* were taken from a recent *cause célèbre*. The contrast is between the idyllic sleepy setting (the *white* cotton) and the tale of blood and avarice (the *red* cotton) there enacted. A further symbolism is implied in the second title, *Turf and Towers*, which oppose the life that drifts at ease to the 'sharpened life' which, as Meredith tells us, 'commands its course.' The hero is another sophist, one Miranda, a Catholic who tries to serve both masters, ease and religion, turf and towers. This converted waster, after a surprising chain of events and reflections, gives a show of sincerity to his madness by flinging himself from the top of the 'tower.' The symbolism weighs the story down. When Browning keeps to sheer sardonic comedy he is excellent, and Molière or Henri Becque might have praised—for its satire, though not for its form—the scene in which Clara, the widow of Miranda, defies all his harpy 'Cousinry' and sits firm in her strong financial position. Despite the squalor of the story, the poet remains genial and almost hopeful at the end of it.

So much cannot be said of *The Inn Album*, where he hardly speaks in person at all. The rascal of the piece, the 'elder man,' predominates; and at one moment he talks exactly like Browning. He exclaims to the woman whom he had betrayed, and who then miserably married a fanatic,

> Let this parenthetic doubt
> Of love, in men, have been the trial-test
> Appointed to all flesh at some one stage
> Of soul's achievement.

This is Satan quoting scripture. But the subtlety lies here, that for once Satan is doing so sincerely; the elder man feels that he has indeed missed the prize of life. By such strokes the villains of Thackeray are outdone; but the *Inn*

VERSE *APOLOGIAS* 53

Album often recalls his novels. There is the same knowledge of the card-room, the club-world, and the half-world. The story is freely adapted from an actual scandal of the last generation, and is too intricate to summarise easily; but the incidents are closely riveted, and the actual ending is the only possible one. All the characters are unnamed. The 'lady' is no lamblike or saintly Pompilia, but magnificent in wrath and denunciation. She was ruined, she fled to a dreary marriage; the 'younger man,' one of Browning's best pictures of manly and primitive youth, has loved and missed her, not knowing that her injurer is the 'elder man,' the very man who has taken him up, initiated him, tried to fleece him, and won his adoration. At the crisis he slays the elder man, and the woman commits suicide. At last, with the two bodies lying before him, he opens the door to a fourth person, the young girl whom he was about to marry and who had sought the counsel of the dead woman. Save for this lightly pencilled figure there is hardly a touch of charm in *The Inn Album*, except one description of an elm-tree:

O you exceeding beauty, bosomful
Of lights and shades, murmurs and silences,
Sun-warmth, dew-coolness—squirrel, bee, and bird,
High, higher, highest, till the blue proclaims

'*Leave earth, there's nothing better till next step Heavenward!*'—so, off flies what has wings to help.

The Inn Album is the last remarkable long poem that Browning wrote. It has discomfited some of his admirers, but had it not been in verse it would have taken its place in fiction. Would that it had not been in verse! It recalls the old 'domestic' tragedies like *Arden of Feversham*, where the passions are left naked and their speech is little transfigured out of the ferocity of fact. Still, Browning throws a fine spume of his own over the most literal language; and the dignity of the injured lady lifts *The Inn Album* out of bare realism.

X

Refreshment with Greek themes : *Balaustion*, etc.
—Also *La Saisiaz*, etc.

Meanwhile he began, for refreshment, to produce his 'transcripts' of Greek stories. So might a man, whilst working in mine or sewer, make holiday in the open-air theatre of Athens or Epidaurus. He could not for ever resist the call of beauty. He began with *Balaustion's Adventure*, where cordiality and song predominate, and hope and goodness flower. The setting was partly suggested by Plutarch; but the girl Balaustion, the 'wild pomegranate-flower,' who chants the *Alcestis* of Euripides to the Syracusans for the redemption of the Grecian captives, is the poet's own invention. She is one of his living and delightful figures. 'Herakles,' whom Euripides had presented in a perplexing light (some scholars believing the intention to be merely derisive), is glorified into a type of the rescuer. His 'great voice,' breaking in upon the keeners in the house of mourning, rather suggests the caricature, now well known, of the solid and ruddy Browning surrounded by a shadowy chorus of dreary persons. The play is 'transcribed,' sometimes roughly and literally, but into close expressive verse, and is commented on by Balaustion-Browning. All is clear and straightforward; the refining over the vacillations of Admetus is part of the problem raised by the original play. Browning wished to defend his wife's favourite Greek poet, and did something to shake the false estimate which had been encouraged by Schlegel in his *Lectures on Dramatic Literature* of 1808. It is plain what Browning owed to Euripides and to Greece. For the moment they cleared his voice, they brought him back to pure beauty.

But beauty does not detain him long: in *Aristophanes's Apology* he is off again into the jungle. The actual version of the *Hercules Furens* has the same virtues as that of the *Alcestis*; and it is even closer, because there are lyrical measures corresponding to those of the original. Balaustion is again the speaker. While sailing to Rhodes with her husband after the downfall of Athens, she dictates to him the story of her conflict with Aristophanes, who had burst into her company upon the news of the death of Euripides. He makes his 'apology' for his attacks on that poet; it is conceived on conservative lines, at the expense of the sophist and eccentric. Balaustion refutes him by reciting the play. The apology bursts into splendour here and there, but is interminable, and choked with crabbed learned allusions and jibes; no Greek would have uttered or listened to it. Aristophanes makes amends when he chants the song of Thamyris, in sweet and flowing *terza rima*. Soon afterwards Browning produced his translation of the *Agamemnon* of Æschylus, which few have praised. The measure is not happy and the style is doggedly literal and strained. The mistake, similar to that which Morris made over *Beowulf*, seems to lie in supposing that an idiom which, though difficult, is natural in one language produces the same effect when it is slavishly followed in another language, where it is not natural and therefore still more difficult. We are far here from the lovely and stately Hellenic of the poet's youth, *Artemis Prologizes*.

Johnson somewhere shakes his head over the task of 'the most vigorous mind when it is employed at once upon argument and poetry'; and in *La Saisiaz*, whatever the fate of the argument, the poetry must be held to suffer. But the overture is a lofty utterance of collected grief. The poet, who had lost his friend and fellow-climber, treads, now alone, the familiar uphill road; and the verse, with its *Locksley Hall* rhymes, echoes his paces. The rest is a plea, exalted in tenor and bleak in language, for the belief in personal survival, without which all human hopes are represented as idle. The Stoical view of the agnostic does not figure among the arguments controverted. Many passages recall Bishop Butler, and Browning gives a new turn to his own favourite idea of life as a probation. The soul requires a troubled progress towards perfection, and this progress can only be consummated in another life. In the same volume, in *The Two Poets of Croisic*, he turns to a lighter mood. This is one of his pleasanter works, with its pensive moral. The poets are historical persons. There is René Gentilhomme, who prophesied truly the birth of a Dauphin, and who was much honoured and then forgotten; and there is Desforges Maillard, who disguised himself as a lady, published his verses in her name, and cheated Voltaire into saluting him gallantly. Here Browning uses the roguish *Don Juan* metre, though he does not make the most of its powers.

XI

Dramatic Idyls; a new form of the 'dramatic romances'—The four last volumes.

He now went back, with a difference, to the lyrical ballad, or story of action. Most of the *Dramatic Idyls* are of this kind, and are also poems of casuistry. He does not deal in obvious morals, and likes to exhibit the trial of courage or piety under extraordinary conditions, when a sudden choice must be made carrying with it either self-acquittal or remorse. But he does not show interest in the mere temptation

To buy the merry madness of one hour
With the long irksomeness of following time.

He must have strange cases; and in one of them, that of *Ivàn Ivànovitch*, a tale which he had heard in Russia in his youth, he surely turns the winch too far. It is the tale of Ivàn's wife, who let the wolves tear her children from her and resisted furiously, but did not fling herself to die with them. For this lapse Ivàn beheads her in public, and the village pope hails him therefore as 'God's servant,' and discourses on the duties of mothers. It may have happened;

but is the sentiment simply dramatic, or does the poet, too, applaud the atrocity of Ivàn? If so, his sympathy is better warranted in the case of *Martin Relph*, where the conscience-stricken speaker is a virtual murderer. *Ned Bratts* is versified from the story of ' Old Tod ' in Bunyan's *Mr. Badman* : Bratts and his wife are slayers and thieves, but are converted, and plunge into court, and confess, and face their sentence. The speech of Bratts is a grimy, fiery, and splendid explosion. In *Halbert and Hob* there is the just and tragic, though not fatal, expiation of a fault ; the father suffers his son to outrage him, just so far as he had outraged his own father long ago, but no further. All these poems are in long rolling rhymes of various pattern. The situation is sharpest and most intricate in *Clive*, where three separate mental crises are presented. Two are actual ; there is the breakdown of the card-sharper, whose pistol Clive, his exposer, calmly faces ; and there is the test of Clive's courage as he does so. But these only lead up to the third crisis, which is imaginary, and which consists in the humiliation which Clive *would* have felt if his enemy, instead of collapsing, had spared him in assumed contempt. The whole setting and performance of this poem, with the figure of the officer listening to Clive's story, is worthy of Browning's prime.

In others of the ' idyls ' there is also a recovery

of charm. Such are the Arab tale of the horse
Muléykeh, and the Greek tales of *Echetlos* and
Pheidippides; and there is all Browning's youthful feeling for beauty in the moon-scenery of *Pan
and Luna,* where the silvery images make us
forget some jars of sound:

And thus it proved when—diving into space,
Stript of all vapour, from each web of mist
Utterly film-free—entered on her race
The naked Moon, full-orbed antagonist
Of night and dark, night's dowry; peak to base,
Upstarted mountains, and each valley, kissed
To sudden life, lay silver-bright; in air
Flew she revealed, Maid-Moon with limbs all bare.

Ixion, which comes in the next volume, *Jocoseria,* is not properly a 'Hellenic'; for the myth
is turned into a scornful condemnation of the
unjust Zeus by the tortured Ixion; who appeals
to the unknown 'Potency' behind the tyrant
in the name of the ideal rights of man. Shelley,
in the 'Demogorgon' of *Prometheus Unbound,*
had personified this court of appeal less successfully. *Jocoseria,* besides the famous and musical
lyric, 'Never the time and the place,' contains
one dramatic monologue. *Cristina and Mon-
aldeschi,* which is a fierce and magnificent exhala-
tion of vengeance planned and satisfied. The
scene, with its streak of diabolic humour, shows
all Browning's pristine power. The craven and
treacherous lover whom the queen draws to the

fatal ambush is solely but sufficiently depicted through the gestures which are described in her narrative. Browning feels an almost savage interest in any kind of coward.

In *Ferishtah's Fancies*, under the guise of an Eastern fabulist, he once more reasons out his faith. Again we learn the significance of earthly pain and penance and the value of obstacles to the aspiring soul. The keynote is the worth of love, as compared with knowledge, in supporting us through the struggle; and it is struck in the inserted lyrics, some of which are very fresh and beautiful. The rest of the book though seldom obscure is crabbedly and barely written, with more than the usual play of quirk and eccentricity. I once saw a treasured note from Browning to a young poet who had sent him verses; wherein, speaking as a veteran 'practitioner,' and perhaps echoing his own Abt Vogler, he noted how some chance gathering of common words may suddenly break into a 'star.' The stars of phrase flash out more rarely in these late volumes, though the force of mind is unabated. *Parleyings with Certain People of Importance in their Day* is full of curious interest and untired play of intellect. The parleyings are with Christopher Smart, Bubb Dodington, the painter Gerard de Lairesse, and other forgotten persons. Some of the similes and descriptions are rich in colour and energy. The body of Smart's poetry is compared to a decent and dreary mansion in which one gorgeous chapel, the *Song to David*, is concealed. In *Gerard de Lairesse* the figure of Artemis is beheld on the sun-steeped mountain after the clearing of the storm, and the clear tints of *Artemis Prologizes* reappear, with a swifter measure and a freer style :

What hope along the hillside, what far bliss
Lets the crisp hair-plaits fall so low they kiss
Those lucid shoulders ?   Must a morn so blithe,
Needs have its sorrow when the twang and hiss
Tell that from out thy sheaf one shaft makes writhe
Its victim, thou unerring Artemis ?

The thinking, no doubt, often swamps the poetry; but the handiwork is still that of a great old age. In the posthumous printed *Asolando* the poet writes his own epitaph, 'One who never turned his back,' a poem which is in the strain of *Prospice*, and which, if less sublime, is not less courageous. Signs of age appear rather in the knotting and gnarling of the language than in any loss of power. *Asolando* also shows a recovered lightness and freshness of mood, and some of the verse positively dances. The double refrain ('Clara, Clara') in *Rosny* recalls the 'Edward, Edward' of the old ballad. *Speculative* is a soaring lyric of the early kind. *Reverie* once more celebrates the trinity of Power, Love, and Faith. 'All these and more come flocking' to prove Browning's unconquerable resilience, one of his greater qualities.

XII

Browning's dealings with words : love of monosyllables ; false stresses ; metrical mastery nevertheless—His grammar ; an example ; its justification.

Tennyson, it has been said, tried to give to English the virtues of Italian. Browning seemed to rejoice in the inherent defects of our language; he liked it to be English to a fault. Not that he was prejudiced like Morris against the 'learned' element in it, or against the legacy of Milton; or had any leaning like Swinburne to the use and abuse of biblical diction. But he has a passion for the monosyllable however much it may creak and grind; and the monosyllable is usually of 'native' origin. Nine times out of ten, when his verse is rough or deterrent, that is the reason. Some of his clusters of consonants—*ndgr, lpsfl, lpss*—recall the names in *Gulliver's Travels:*

  Let us not always say
   ' Spite of this flesh to-day
I strove, made head, gai*ned g*round upon the
   whole ! '
  As the bird wings and sings,
   Let us cry ' All good things
Are ours, nor soul he*lps fl*esh more, now, than
   flesh he*lps s*oul.'

Such a style, which comes to its acme in *Dramatis
Personæ*, is well and duly parodied in Swinburne's
Heptalogia; but then it is often the right and
necessary style. For the discords are wanted
in the service of an intense or an exalted mood
which is fully conscious of the past or present
struggle involved in its attainment; and no
easier style would serve. And the technique
of the verse is affected by this congestion of
consonants and monosyllables; the result being
many 'spondees,' and a slow hindered march
which has its own music of a subtle kind:

> Táke the clóak from his fáce, and at fírst
> Lèt the córpse dò its wórst.
>
> Hòw he líes in his ríghts of a mán!
> Deáth has dóne àll deàth cán . . .

Not infrequently, and above all in the 'ana-
pæstic' measures of which Browning is otherwise
a master, he falsifies the natural accent. Yet he
goes on joyously over snags and boulders; and
whether as rough-rider, or when guiding his
smooth-pacing Arab, his *Muléykeh*, he is still a
master-horseman. His invention and his control
of metre are surprising, and to the last he is ever
finding new tunes. The slow suave undula-
tions of *Rudel*; the piercing simple cadences of
White Witch-craft; galloping measures, choppy
measures, stately measures, all are there. But

to enlarge on this would be to repeat what has been well said by others. The extremes of Browning's power and weakness, of his roughness and smoothness, are to be found in his blank verse.

Something, however, may be added on his grammar and idiom, which have certain constant features. They are, as with Shakespeare, the expression of life and impulse; and, even with the precedent of the Grammarian, it may seem mere pedantry to think of 'properly basing' them. It is not pedantry; but the subject would need a tractate. Some peculiarities lie on the surface. We need not fear the curses launched in *Pacchiarotto* 'against the 'ignorance, impudence, envy, and malice' of verbal critics; for the inquiry, on the whole, tells in Browning's honour.

Was it 'grammar' wherein you would 'coach' me—
You—pacing in even that paddock
Of language allotted you *ad hoc*,
With a clog at your fetlocks,—you—scorners
Of me free of all its four corners?

And Browning's grammar is not so much false as free. It represents an effort to show that for all the work of the 'classical' and succeeding ages English syntax is still ductile in the right hands. Carlyle made a similar effort, and for all his incidental contortions prevailed. Browning

is one of the few English poets since Milton who
may be said to have a grammar of his own. He
is strong enough to have one. It is no doubt
hit or miss with him. But the grammar is much
the same throughout ; it is a deliberately practised
idiom that soon becomes second nature. Some
features of it may be noticed in a single passage
of his ' parleying ' with Christopher Smart :

                                   Such success
Befell Smart only out of throngs between
Milton and Keats that donned the singing-dress—
Smart, solely of such songmen, pierced the screen
'Twixt thing and word, lit language straight from
    soul—
Left no fine film flake on the naked coal
Live from the censer—shapely or uncouth,
Fire-suffused through and through, one blaze
    of truth
Undeadened by a lie ;—(you have my mind)—
For, think ! this blaze outleapt with black behind
And blank before, when Hayley and the rest . . .
But let the dead successors worst and best
Bury their dead : with life be my concern—
Yours with the fire-flame : what I fain would
    learn
Is just—(suppose me haply ignorant
Down to the common knowledge, doctors vaunt)
Just this—why only once the fire-flame was . . .

Nothing can be unliker the traditional poetic
paragraph, or ' period,' either grammatically or
musically : it is natural, broken speech plunging
forward, rather fettered by its rhymes, and

straining to be blank verse. Also there is a deliberate omission of articles, which is most marked in passages that require discords and thudding spondees. A similar effect is heard in *Shop* :

> Then off made buyer with a prize,
>   Then seller to his ' Times ' returned
> And so did day wear, wear, till eyes
>   Brightened apace, for rest was earned :
>   He locked door long ere candle burned.

There is the omission of the relative pronoun—again for *staccato* effect; the free use of the breathless dash, appositive or transitional; and of the absolute clause, and of parenthesis. And alliteration is heaped for the enhancement, or at the cost, of melody. So we might, it is plain, proceed; the total effect being that of an interrupted stumbling gallop, of a concision that causes delay, and of a strange rough harmony emerging at the last. And the special idioms of Caliban, of Bishop Blougram, and of Dominus Hyacinthus are imposed upon these rude elements. Calverley's parody in *The Cock and the Bull* is full of such scholarship. For Browning, on the whole, makes good his grammar and syntax, as George Meredith, on the whole, does not. We can ' learn his great language,' and honourably salute it, though with occasional amusement. The philosopher Shadworth Hodgson[n] well says that 'this dependence of the syntactical construction upon the context' is what 'compels the reader to be constantly interpreting the parts by the whole instead of the whole by the parts, and constitutes, as it seems to me, the peculiar beauty and the peculiar difficulty of Mr. Browning's style.'

XIII

His non-poetical element—Philosophic verse; creation of characters and types; power greatest in lyric—His men and women—Neutral ground between prose and verse—Browning's quality.

He wrote reams of verse which are not poetry, though poetry is always struggling to appear. He seems to have been little aware of its absence, like Chapman and many a good Elizabethan. He had a similar contempt for the public and the critics, although like Tennyson he was always angrily thinking about them. But this is only to say that Browning's mental force and alertness outrange, as often happens with Englishmen of genius, his artistic power. He tried to put into poetry much that should never have gone into verse. It is not true, though Swinburne said it, that Browning is rapid rather than obscure. He can be so obscure as to annul the value of the thought which he less than half conveys. He breaks his fingers on what is stronger than the strongest man, namely, the genius of the language. He often commits himself to impossible forms and moulds, as in *Sordello* and *Hohenstiel-Schwangau*; some of

CHARACTERISTICS—PHILOSOPHY 71

these long poems are altogether miscreations. Yet this was but the excess and diversion of strength, and Browning's body of living and consummate work is none the worse for failures that lie outside it.

He has reasoned and philosophised in verse more than any English poet of equal gifts. Much has been written on his theology and its 'optimism.' His fervent instinctive theism encouraged the myth that he was of Hebrew blood. It is united with an intense if undoctrinal belief in personal immortality, and with an equally undogmatic and mystical reverence for Christ, whose features he draws after the Fourth Gospel. He so far attends to current controversies as to dismiss certain lurid tenets. In the satire of *Caliban upon Setebos*, and in the *Inn Album* and *Ixion*, the doctrine of reprobation is itself cast forth unto reprobation. The faith in an after-life proclaimed in *La Saisiaz* repudiates the conception of reward and punishment as sapping the moral impulse of man on this earth, who is no longer disinterested if he is to be bribed or threatened. Browning's appeal is always moral and imaginative rather than strictly philosophical. We must look for his powers in *Abt Vogler* and in *Rabbi Ben Ezra*, in the musings of Pope Innocent, in *Prospice*, and in the *Epilogue* to *Asolando*. Luckily it is here that he is most of a poet; and when he is once fairly launched few have equalled him in energy and security of style. His execution at its best does not fall behind his spirit of faith and courage. Whatever we may think of his faith, he has done the utmost for its expression. The optimist, at the worst, has had a great innings; and his knowledge of human nature, of traps and pitfalls and stumblings and of the enemy generally, has saved him from too cheap assertion. And he is always best when he chants his sermon. Start where we will with Browning, we come back at last to his lyrical gift.

The web of circumstance and situation in his world, I began by saying, is very tough and definite; and he gives the taste of life, with its oddity, colour, and splendour, as sharply as any poet, whenever he likes. The pictures of Caliban and the Bishop of St. Praxed's and Bratts and a score of others cannot be outdone in their intense expression of temperament. Down into the pit of realism, below the sphere of poetry, yet making a kind of poetry out of what he finds, Browning often plunges, with a dramatic sympathy that seems to be rather intensified by his moral repulsion (indulgence or complicity being far from him). But short of this he moves joyously above ground, with a certain good-natured impatient contempt for the average nature and also a clear vision of it; the contempt

CHARACTERISTICS—PERSONAGES

distinguishing him from Shakespeare, as it does from Chaucer, to whom Landor compared him. His world is amply peopled. Yet with whom, or with what? He has more dramatic sense than any poet of his time; but which of his characters have got into the general memory? Possibly Pippa, or Pompilia; more probably Mr. Sludge. No one else, despite all those brains and pains! There is no Hamlet, no Satan; certainly not even a 'new Don Juan'! It may be said that this test is too severe, and that Browning speaks to the lettered public. But his 'Karshish, Cleon, Norbert, and the fifty,' for all their liveliness and eloquence, are hardly persons. Some, indeed are types not to be forgotten, and Guido and Fra Lippo are more than that. And it is a great thing to create types, as Chaucer created them. But Browning's men are often voices of his own ideas on love and art and faith; and they are little more, for all the colour and detail that surround them. They are from this point of view wonderful inventions. His women are more real and satisfactory, especially when they speak for themselves. They theorise less; and sometimes, like the lady in *The Inn Album*, they have a poetic reality. Sometimes they are lasting types, like the speaker in *Any Wife to Any Husband*. But his usual aim is to present situation and passion rather than to draw persons. It is anybody's passion, anybody's thought with a shadowy thinker behind it. From 1842 to 1890, from *Through the Metidja* to *Dubiety*, a poem in the *Asolando* volume, he retains this power, which gives him his surest title-deeds. He keeps the tones of a perennial youth, which is not like that of Tithonus:

> Perhaps but a memory, after all!
> —Of what came once when a woman leant
> To feel for my brow where her kiss might fall.
> Truth ever, truth only the excellent!

There is much, then, in Browning which is not exactly poetry but is all the same well worth having. It may be good and entertaining of the *Ingoldsby* kind, like the beginning of *Holy Cross Day* ('Fee, faw, fum! bubble and squeak,' etc.). More often it is in blank verse, and in the nature of rapid, allusive, and sarcastic narrative or *apologia*. Much of *The Ring and the Book*, and most of *The Inn Album*, is of this kind. The level is that of very animated prose, but the style is a new invention—cynical, broken, conversational, crutching itself quite effectively upon the metre:

> And did I spoil sport, pull face grim,—nay, grave?
> Your pupil does you better credit! No!
> I parleyed with my pass-book, rubbed my pair
> At the big balance in my banker's hands,
> Folded a cheque cigar-case-shape,—just wants

CHARACTERISTICS—HIS PERSONAGES

Filing and signing,—and took train, resolved
To execute myself with decency
And let you win,—if not Ten thousand quite,
Something by way of wind-up-farewell burst
Of fire-work nosegay!

When he likes Browning can always spurt up from such a level into real poetry; or again can slip into a more agreeable, easy kind of verse-talk. In *The Inn Album* this variety abounds and is delightful. There is one allusion to ' poor hectic Cowper,' and the history of the ' Night-Cap ' suggests, perhaps intentionally, the manner of *The Task*:

> And so, encroaching more and more
> It lingers long past the abstemious meal
> Of morning, and, as prompt to serve, precedes
> The supper-summons, gruel grown a feast.

All this brings us back to our starting-point: Browning's normality, sanity, humanity. He is a man of the world, in the best and strongest sense of the term; his genius has its stubborn roots in real life. And as to his whole performance, we may look on it as on some metal-worker's or lapidary's story, stocked with rubies and chrysolites of the best, and with rings and armlets ' justifiably golden,' and also with the same things half-wrought and ill set, and again with ' cradles ' of the unwashed, gold-containing rubble; one and all being paraded, as if they were the regalia, with a queer unconsciousness of differences. This large absence of self-criticism is one thing that makes Browning so big, so attractive, so Elizabethan. He talked endlessly about art, but hardly knew when he was an artist and when he was not, leaving us to state the matter as best we may.

XIV

Mrs. Browning: life and literary record; faults to be expected.

The early reputation of Elizabeth Barrett was made by two volumes published before her marriage, *The Seraphim and Other Poems* and the *Poems* of 1844. The first of these contained not only highly-pitched romantic lyric like *Margret*, and romantic narrative like *Isobel's Child*, but some less ambitious verse of finer workmanship, mostly reminiscent, such as *An Island, The Deserted Garden, The Sea-Mew*, and *My Doves*; while the most popular as well as the most impassioned piece, though not the surest in note, was *Cowper's Grave*. In the *Poems* of 1844 the scope is wider, the hand less uncertain, and the intensity greater; it contains *The Cry of the Children*, and *Catarina to Camoens*, and *Wine of Cyprus*; but the form, while often beautiful and melodious, is seldom sustained. There are more romances, like the overcharged *Lady Geraldine's Courtship*, and pleasant simple things like the lines *To Flush, My Dog*; who, she observes in a letter, 'understands Greek excellently well.' But work like *A Rhapsody of Life's*

Progress again shows the authoress on a false track; within a few years she was to find a truer one. Meanwhile in 1844, she contributed a fervent essay on Carlyle and a good deal of other matter to *A New Spirit of the Age,* by the poet Horne, the writer of *Orion.*

Miss Barrett's marriage to Robert Browning in 1846 did not merely bring her renewed health and personal happiness after an invalided and hermit life; it was also a release from prison. Her father's notion of the *patria potestas* in the article of marriage amounted to a monomania, and the wedding took place without his knowledge. It enabled Mrs. Browning to escape from London to Italy, and from a sofa surrounded with books to the great world, Browning's 'world of men,' of public affairs, and of vital ideas: and she herself was afterwards to write:

> I lived with visions for my company
> Instead of men and women, years ago.

The letters exchanged between Browning and Miss Barrett were published after both were dead; they do nothing but honour to both writers, of course; yet the reader is shy of over-hearing love-letters; and another record of this fortunate union was given to the world by the poetess in her *Sonnets from the Portuguese.* They come not from the Portuguese, but from the soul of the writer, and often attain a purity of form worthy of their splendid inspiration. Like the nightingale, Mrs. Browning was 'a creature of a fiery heart.'

The Brownings lived and wrote in Italy, their second country, making occasional flights to England. They chiefly lived in Florence, and Mrs. Browning's next book, *Casa Guidi Windows*, is the record of a sanguine, absorbed onlooker, vehement in sympathy with the Italian cause and nourishing an admiration, afterwards to be chilled, for Louis Napoleon. It is most unequal in execution but alive with observation and enthusiasm. Then adventuring on blank verse, Mrs. Browning produced the long story, *Aurora Leigh*, which succeeded, but which is now somewhat stranded. Many of the *Poems before Congress* are political rather than poetical. But the posthumous volume of 1862 contains some of Mrs. Browning's best writings, including *Bianca among the Nightingales*, and one triumph in dramatic monologue, *Lord Walter's Wife*. The influence of her husband's *Dramatic Lyrics*, for good and ill, can be traced here; the style is stronger, and the grasp of situation too; but Browning's ruggedness does not sit well upon her looser habit of speech.

There have been few good poetesses at any time or in any country. Among those who have written in English, it is equally certain that Mrs. Browning is not the surest artist and that she 'has the largest and most comprehensive soul.' She deserves her husband's praises so well, that it is an ungrateful business to criticise her strictly. *One Word More*, and the 'posy' in *The Ring and the Book*, and *By the Fireside*, considered as a description of Mrs. Browning's spirit and nature, do not lead to disappointment when we turn to her own poetry. Her performance it is well to approach with some critical precautions. It would be a mistake, within a week of doing so, to read either Robert Browning or Christina Rossetti; and it is best, perhaps, to begin with a prejudice of the right kind, in order to find how often it is disarmed. Prepare from the first to come almost anywhere on a lapse of language into almost every fault except vulgarity, or on a vicious rhyme or a defect of rhythm, or on queer vague matter, diffuse and high-flown, or on hectic writing. Expect all this—and again and again you will *not* find it; but will come on passages of melody unbroken and imagery unimpaired; on gorgeous things, and also on simple things, which are successful and leave you free to admire the generous poetic vision that inspires them. Had Mrs. Browning written more things like the *Sonnets from the Portuguese* she might have ranked with a poet like Rossetti, and not, as she does rank, with another great but unequal sonneteer, Sir Philip Sidney. The parallel is less odd than it may sound. In both writers there is the same intermittence and the same occasional triumph; and both of them frequently leave us with the sense of a rightness that has only just gone wrong. Both, too, have the power of recovery, and are always liable to be excellent.

XV

Nature; and the Greek poets—False rhymes.

Mrs. Browning from her youth up had a passion for nature and also for the Greek poets. The copses and orchards, the rich fat rolling scenery, breaking into steepness, of the countryside lying below the Malverns on their Herefordshire flank, are heard of in her early writings; nor did Italy ever make her forget them. These Ledbury verses include *The Lost Bower, The Deserted Garden,* and others already named; also the pretty *Hector in the Garden*:

> Underneath the chestnuts dripping,
>   Through the grasses wet and fair,
>   Straight I sought my garden-ground
>   With the laurel on the mound,
> And the pear-tree oversweeping
>   A side-shadow of green air.
>
> In the garden lay supinely
>   A huge giant wrought of spade! . . .

The giant is the figure of Hector wrought in flowers, and the child dreams that perhaps the soul of the real Hector may enter into the giant. For more work like this, who would not give away all Mrs. Browning's Byronic or spasmodic compositions like *The Seraphim* and *A Drama of Exile*, and some of her romances too? But we must not ignore *Margret* with its complaining music and deftly varied refrain. Mrs. Browning was fond of the refrain; but it is a dangerous device, for while a good refrain may save, a bad one will damn, almost any poem in the world. The nightingales, singing at the end of each verse in *Bianca*, sing aright; but the repetition of the words *Toll slowly* in the *Lay of the Brown Rosary* only tempts us to say with Othello, ' Silence that dreadful bell '! Yet, again, the burden of *The Dead Pan* is a true close, and aptly fitted to every stanza: *Pan, Pan is Dead*. This piece is the best fruit of Mrs. Browning's Greek studies, which claim separate mention.

She read the poets honestly in the originals, from Homer to Gregory Nazianzen, and in her *Wine of Cyprus* recites their praises with much colour, gaiety, and ardour. It is her happiest piece of familiar verse, and alludes to her readings with her blind instructor, Hugh Stuart Boyd. The memory of the same scholar is honoured afterwards in three sonnets, of which the last, entitled *Legacies*, is of great beauty. The Greeks did not teach Mrs. Browning their own virtues of form; but she has her place beside the transcriber of the *Alcestis* among the poetic humanists of the period. Her dealings with ' our Æschylus, the thunderous' were, indeed, not much more fortunate than her husband's. She produced, and deplored, a youthful version of the *Prometheus*, and afterwards made another one. Her essay on *The Greek Christian Poets* contains many translations, and is a scampering review of an enthusiastic though not uncritical kind. Her *Book of the Poets* is a similar style and full of eager enjoyment. The poets are the English poets, and the list closes with Wordsworth, whose reputation was now established. His influence is sometimes traceable in Mrs. Browning; and that to advantage, as in the charming piece called *An Island*. *A Vision of Poets* is the counterpart in verse to the *Book of the Poets*. It contains a happy characterisation of Chaucer, and also of Ossian, ' once counted greater than the rest,' and some true Tennysonian scenery:

A wild brown moorland underneath,
And four pools breaking up the heath
With white low gleamings, blank as death.

There is nothing to be said for Mrs. Browning's deliberate way of rhyming falsely whenever she is minded to do so. She says that it is the ' result not of carelessness, but of conviction, and indeed of much patient study of the great masters of English.' Nothing has hurt her reputation more; but the precise nature and extent of her error must be remembered. It occurs chiefly in her early works, rather than in the *Sonnets from the Portuguese* or in *Casa Guidi Windows*. It is often found where she is courting the difficulties of double rhyme. English has its traditional freedoms, which are somewhat boldly extended by Dante Rossetti. In *The Blessed Damozel* are to be found: *untrod, God, cloud,* and *mild, fill'd smil'd.* This is ' consonance ' : the vowel is deserted, while the consonant-sounds following are retained. Mrs. Browning goes further, and passes bounds with her *mortal, turtle ; altars, welters ; moonshine, sunshine.* Assonance (which is the retention of the vowel, while the following consonant-sounds are altered) she also uses, but not so freely, although she is commonly reproached with ' assonances.' Such are : *benches, Influences; Nazianzen, glancing ; trident, silent.* But sometimes she combines both processes, and two examples will probably suffice the reader : *angels, candles ; panther, saunter.* Such practices are the more to be deplored because they often introduce the effect of ' a brazen canstick turned or a dry wheel grating ' in the midst of an otherwise excellent melody. The effect is such that no writer of any credit since Mrs. Browning has tried to imitate it.

XVI

Sonnets from the Portuguese, Casa Guidi Windows, Aurora Leigh.

The forty-four *Sonnets from the Portuguese* form a sequence, or continuous poem, written in a state of happiness, but mostly ringing the changes on a single theme, namely, the writer's sense of humility; with a standing contrast between her present condition and her former one of loneliness and seclusion. The tone is now and then lighter, as befits her joyful estate, and then it runs into playful images and conceits; 'The soul's Rialto hath its merchandise'; and there is a strange flight of this kind in the thirty-seventh sonnet. Here, in the sestet, she exclaims that she can set up only an unworthy counterfeit of her love, even as a 'shipwrecked Pagan safe in port,' might set up, instead of 'his guardian sea-god,' a 'sculptured porpoise.' This, however, is cheerfulness breaking through. The prevailing note of these poems is so high, the spirit so ardent, and the matter so intimate, that they might seem to claim immunity from inspection. Still, the sonnet-form is the most exacting of all; and, besides, Mrs. Browning published

SONNETS FROM THE PORTUGUESE

the book. Everywhere there is the same spiritual fire ; none of the sonnets are without beauty ; and four or five of them approach the standard of finish which is set by the great, unforgettable examples in the language. They are all in the Italian form, which is observed with due care as regards the rhyme-arrangement, and with some regularity as regards the exact distribution of the thought among the metrical sections. One of the best-wrought is the fifth, where the single image of the ashes of the heart, poured from the sepulchral urn and smouldering at the feet of the beloved but flaming up in his face under the passionate gust of wind, is perfectly carried through. The sonnet itself flames up in the last words, ' Stand farther off then ! go.' Of the other three that are perhaps the best, the fourteenth (' If thou must love me ') has designedly the high Elizabethan ring, in spite of its orthodox versification. The most lofty and magnificent, the twenty-second, ' When our two souls,' is as definitely modern in cast, and the most suggestive of Dante Rossetti. The forty-third, ' How do I love thee ? ' is a much more even, quiet, and regular piece, and may be thought to have the honours in point of depth and simplicity. A commentary on the *Sonnets from the Portuguese* may be found in the small group of companion-lyrics—in which the style of Robert Browning may be detected—called *Insufficiency, Inclusions,*

Proof and Disproof. Whatever their flaws, the *Sonnets from the Portuguese* stand, by right of feeling—and frequently by right of workmanship—apart from other English sonnet series and above most of them.

The first and longer part of *Casa Guidi Windows* records the spectacle of Florence in 1848, when the Grand Duke Leopold made his promise, which came to nothing, of a liberal constitution. The second part written three years later is a generous but turbid tirade, telling of the flight of Leopold and of his return under the protection of Austrian bayonets. The spirit is now one of bitter disenchantment. There is more poetry in the first part; and though the digressions on art are a kind of caricature of *Andrea del Sarto* and *Old Pictures in Florence*, the actual diary of things seen—the procession in the streets, the banners, the impassioned crowd—is admirably written. This was a new venture for Mrs. Browning; as her letters show, she had an eye for a pageant in its colour and detail, and for popular traits and gestures; and it is a pity that she did not oftener write in this style. The poem is in a breathless measure; the stanzas of six run on unbrokenly, and the melody is only occasional; and the general effect is sadly confused.

Aurora Leigh, though a curious document of the time, is, it must be confessed, something of

a ' chokepear ' for the reader of to-day. It is a
long story, laced with long discourses and filling
four hundred pages of blank verse. Like *The
Cry of the Children* it is a proof of Mrs. Browning's
deep humanitarian feeling and of her large heart.
Aurora Leigh is full of the sentiment which
animates Carlyle and Dickens, Ruskin and
Kingsley. We watch the overflow into literature
of the quickened sympathy for the poor and the
dispossessed, and of a noble indignation against
the more cruel and irrational social taboos. The
real heroine, Marian Erle, a sacrificed, innocent
daughter of the people, gives up her betrothed,
the exalted philanthropist Romney Leigh, sooner
than drag him down to her level, and then she
vanishes. Aurora Leigh, his cousin, the woman
of letters, who has watched the story and be-
friended Marian, in the end accepts Romney.
None of these persons are very vivid, and we have
the painful sense that much good emotion has
been wasted on a crowd of shadows. The endless
preaching, arguing, and moral philosophising is
almost as trying as anything in George Eliot.
The verse is prosaic and high-pitched in turn,
as in work of this kind it is bound or doomed
to be. Yet here, as in *Casa Guidi Windows*, we
are aware that in Mrs. Browning there are more
than the makings of a poetic observer. The
best parts of *Aurora Leigh* are the domestic
scenes and the scraps of natural talk. The

speeches of Marian Erle herself, being the simplest, are the best of all. But in form, and temper, and purpose the poem dates itself in the most singular way; and it is needless to echo that stray fling of FitzGerald, which drove Browning to such a burst of fury; seeing that, whether we thank the powers for it or not, there *will* ' be no more *Aurora Leighs.*'

Altogether, we leave Mrs. Browning with a mixture of admiration and discomfort. Her faults of form and phrase are never the faults of smallness; it would have been an honour to have known her. Often we feel we would rather have known her than read her; this is when the faults become too disastrous. But it is good to dwell on her life as well as on the golden and exceptional passages of her verse.

CHRONOLOGICAL TABLE

(Dates are of publication, unless otherwise noted.)

1809. March 6, Elizabeth Barrett born. Childhood at Ledbury : early devotion to scenery, poetry, and the classics.

1812. May 7, Robert Browning, born in Camberwell, son of Robert Browning, of the Bank of England, and his wife (born Wiedemann). Irregular schooling and precocious self-education. Residence with parents till 1846 ; intervals of travel.

1833. The Barretts go to London. Browning visits Russia ; and, 1834, Italy.

1833. *Pauline* (anonymous). Miss Barrett : translation of Æschylus, *Prometheus Vinctus*, with some original poems.

1835. *Paracelsus.* 1836. *Porphyria's Lover* and *Johannes Agricola in Meditation* (published as *Madhouse Cells*).

1837. *Strafford* played by Macready.

1838. Visit to Italy. Miss Barrett : *The Seraphim and Other Poems.*

1840. *Sordello. King Victor and King Charles*, included in

1841-6. *Bells and Pomegranates,* eight series (in Nos. iii and vii are the first dramatic lyrics and romances) containing the plays : *Pippa Passes, The Return of the Druses, A Blot on the 'Scutcheon* (acted 1843), *Colombe's Birthday* (acted 1853), *Luria, A Soul's Tragedy,* and *In a Balcony*. Growing note amongst men of letters ; friendships with Carlyle, Tennyson, and others.

1843. Miss Barrett: *The Cry of the Children*, in *Blackwood's*, and contributions to *A New Spirit of the Age* (prose papers), by R. H. Horne.
1844. Miss Barrett: *Poems* (including *Lady Geraldine's Courtship*).
1845. First correspondence and meeting of Browning with Miss Barrett. Her seclusion as an invalid, under parental tyranny.
1846. Sept. 12, secret marriage with Miss Barrett at St. Marylebone Church. The Brownings depart for Italy.
1847–1861. Headquarters chiefly at Casa Guidi, Florence, with visits to Pisa, Siena, etc., and to Paris and England.
1847. Mrs. Browning: *Sonnets from the Portuguese*, published at Reading.
1849. First edition of Browning's *Collected Poems*, 2 vols.
1850. *Christmas Eve and Easter Day*. Mrs. Browning: *Poems*.
1851. Mrs. Browning: *Casa Guidi Windows*; interest in Florentine and Italian politics.
1852. *Essay on Shelley*, prefixed to *Letters* (later found to be spurious) of Shelley.
1855. *Men and Women* (i.e. the 'fifty poems finished,' with *One Word More*; the title later covered only thirteen poems, the rest being scattered under 'dramatic romances,' and 'dramatic lyrics.')
1856. Mrs. Browning: *Aurora Leigh*.
1859. The Brownings take care of Walter Savage Landor.
1860. Mrs. Browning: *Poems before Congress*.
1861. June 30, Death of Mrs. Browning, and burial, in Florence. Return of Browning to London with his son.
1862. Mrs. Browning's *Last Poems*.
1863. Mrs. Browning's essays, *The Greek Christian Poets*.
1864. *Dramatis Personæ*.

1868-9. *The Ring and the Book*, four vols.
1871-7. Greek studies: *Balaustion's Adventure, a Transcript from Euripides (Alcestis); Aristophanes' Apology* (contains Euripides, *Hercules Furens*); and translation of Æschylus, *Agamemnon*.
1871-5. Long poems: *Prince Hohenstiel-Schwangau, a Saviour of Society. Fifine at the Fair.* Two on crime: *Red Cotton Nightcap-Country; The Inn Album.*
1876. *Pacchiarotto, and How he Worked in Distemper.*
1878. *La Saisiaz*, and *The Two Poets of Croisic.*
1878-9. *Dramatic Idyls*, two series; revival of lyrical and dramatic gift.
1881. Browning Society founded by Frederick James Furnivall and Miss E. H. Hickey: many publications, down to 1890.
1879-1886. Many academic and other honours.
1883-1890. *Jocoseria. Ferishtah's Fancies. Parleyings with Certain People of Importance in their Day. Asolando* (posthumous, 1890).
1889. Visit to Asolo.
1890. Dec. 12, death at Vénice. Burial in Westminster Abbey.

NOTES

ROBERT BROWNING

i. *Biography.* The fullest *Life* is by W. Hall Griffin, completed by H. C. Minchin, 1910; and see the *Life and Letters*, by Mrs. Sutherland Orr, as revised by Sir F. G. Kenyon, 1908. *Letters of Robert Browning and E. B. Barrett, 1845-6*, 2 vols., 1899. Lady Ritchie (Miss Thackeray), *Records of Tennyson, Ruskin, Browning*, 1892.

ii. *Writings.* Centenary edition, 10 vols., 1912, introductions by Sir F. G. Kenyon. Many other editions, e.g. in 2 vols., 1896, etc.

iii. *Comment.* This is very abundant. There is no better brief guide than Arthur Symons, *Introduction to Browning* (revised ed., 1906). For a work of reference, see E. Berdoe, *Browning Cyclopædia*, 1892. More continuous studies, all of value, are by: G. K. Chesterton, 1903 ('English Men of Letters'); E. Dowden, 1904; C. H. Herford, 1905; and E. Berger (1912), in *Grands Écrivains étrangers*. Those who have access to the *Papers* of the Browning Society (1881-1895) will find instructive matter by F. J. Furnivall, J. T. Nettleship, and others (e.g. on *Sordello*). On metres, see G. Saintsbury, *Hist. of Eng. Prosody*, 1910, iii. 216-240.

p. 9. *Bells and Pomegranates.* See Exodus xxviii., 33, 34.

p. 44. *The Ring and the Book.* The original 'yellow book,' now in Balliol College Library, has been reproduced photographically, with translation and commentary, by C. W. Hodell, *The Old Yellow Book*, 1908 (Carnegie Institution, Washington); and the substance of this is given in *The Old Yellow Book*, 1911 (Everyman's Library).

p. 68. Shadworth Hodgson. The passage is in his *Theory of Practice*, 1870, ii. 272 ff.

MRS. BROWNING

i. *Biography*. *Letters*. ed. Sir F. G. Kenyon, 2 vols., 1897; and her *Letters* as Miss Barrett, cited above. J. K. Ingram, *Elizabeth Barrett Browning*, 1888, in 'Eminent Women Series.'

ii. *Writings*. Complete *Poems*, 1904, 2 vols. and 1· vol.

iii. *Comment*. On *Aurora Leigh*, see Joseph Texte, *Études de Littérature européenne*, 1898, pp. 239-277. On Mrs. Browning's rhymes, see her own defence in Kenyon, *Letters*, i. 182-3; and G. Saintsbury, *Hist. of Eng. Prosody*, iii. 241-8.